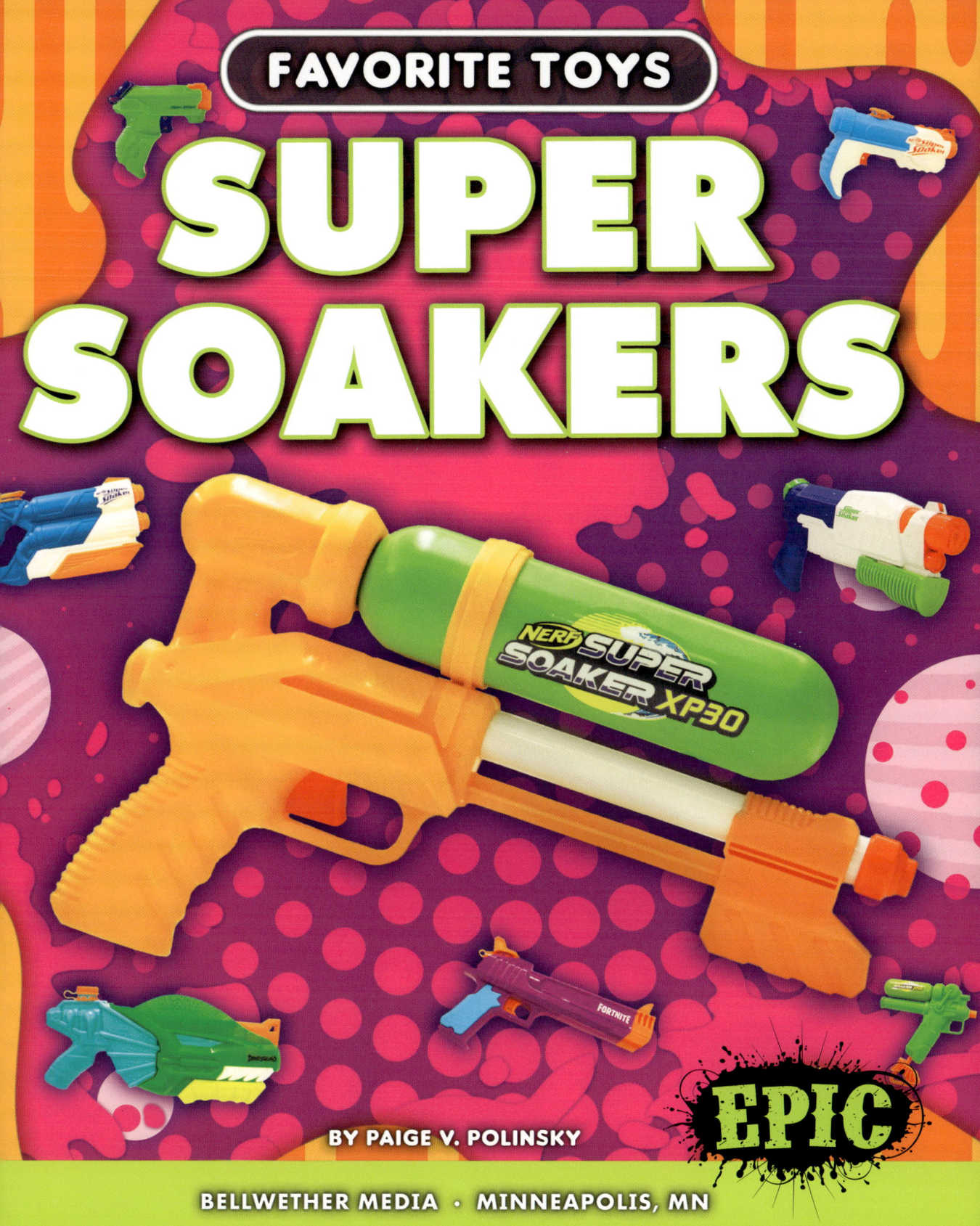

EPIC

Action and adventure collide in EPIC. Plunge into a universe of powerful beasts, hair-raising tales, and high-speed excitement. Astonishing explorations await. Can you handle it?

This is not an official Nerf book. It is not approved by or connected with Hasbro, Inc.

This edition first published in 2023 by Bellwether Media, Inc.

No part of this publication may be reproduced in whole or in part without written permission of the publisher. For information regarding permission, write to Bellwether Media, Inc., Attention: Permissions Department, 6012 Blue Circle Drive, Minnetonka, MN 55343.

LC record for Super Soakers available at: https://lccn.loc.gov/2022004844

Text copyright © 2023 by Bellwether Media, Inc. EPIC and associated logos are trademarks and/or registered trademarks of Bellwether Media, Inc.

Editor: Elizabeth Neuenfeldt   Designer: Josh Brink

Printed in the United States of America, North Mankato, MN.

TABLE OF CONTENTS

Wetter Is Better!......................4
The History of......................6
   Super Soakers
Super Soakers Today............14
More Than a Toy....................18
Glossary..............................22
To Learn More....................23
Index..................................24

Wetter Is Better!

A boy runs across warm grass. His brother chases him. It is the Super Soaker battle of the summer!

Suddenly, the boy turns around. They both fire. Splash! These Soakers are a super way to beat the heat!

The History of Super Soakers

Lonnie Johnson **invented** the Super Soaker in Nebraska in 1982. At first, he was trying to build a new heat pump.

THE PROFESSOR

LONNIE BEGAN INVENTING AS A CHILD. HIS NICKNAME WAS "THE PROFESSOR"!

LONNIE JOHNSON

SUPER SOAKER BEGINNINGS

**Offutt Air Force Base
Omaha, Nebraska =** 🔴

When Lonnie connected the pump to his sink, water shot out. It soaked his bathroom!

Lonnie's water gun was stronger than others. It used a **trigger** to blast water nearly 40 feet (12 meters)!

MASTER BLASTER

NERF BLASTERS

LONNIE LATER INVENTED THE NERF BLASTER DART GUN. HE BASED IT ON THE SUPER SOAKER!

Lonnie looked for a company to sell his toy. In 1989, the Larami **Corporation** agreed to help.

Lonnie's water gun hit stores in 1990. It was called the Power Drencher.

To boost sales, Larami changed the name to Super Soaker. TV **ads** got the word out. In 1991, 2 million Super Soakers sold!

In 1994, XP Soakers were made. They had bigger **nozzles**. Some even had two or three! The Constant Pressure System Super Soakers came out in 1996. They could shoot 30 ounces (887 milliliters) of water in one second!

XP SOAKER

CONSTANT PRESSURE SYSTEM SUPER SOAKER

SUPER SOAKER TIMELINE

1982
Lonnie Johnson invents the Super Soaker

1990
The first Super Soaker is sold in stores as the Power Drencher

1991
The toy is renamed the Super Soaker

1996
The first Constant Pressure System Super Soaker is released

2015
The Super Soaker enters the National Toy Hall of Fame

Super Soakers Today

Today, Super Soakers are sold by Hasbro. Like Hasbro's Nerf blasters, many Soakers have **scopes**. Some Soakers have water drums. Players can carry extra water on the go!

A FLOOD OF FUN

AROUND 175 DIFFERENT TYPES OF SUPER SOAKERS HAVE BEEN MADE!

SUPER SOAKER TYPES

DinoSquad

Freezefire

Fortnite HC-E

Scatter Strike

Water fights are fun for all ages. New Soakers come out nearly every year!

16

FORTNITE RL SUPER SOAKER

EXTREME SOAKAGE!
ARROSAGE EXTRÊME!
¡EMPAPADA EXTREMA!
ENCHARCAMENTO EXTREMO.

SUPER FAN

WATER GUN COLLECTOR CHRIS REID OWNS 340 SUPER SOAKERS!

Some are based on the video game *Fortnite*. Fans can use their favorite blasters in real life!

More Than a Toy

Super Soakers bring people together. In 2015, Gabriel Nyantakyi created Waterarms Over **Firearms**. It hosts water fights in Pennsylvania. People also use Soakers at the Songkran Festival. It is the world's biggest water fight!

SONGKRAN FESTIVAL PROFILE

What Is It? The world's biggest water fight

What Does It Celebrate? The start of the Buddhist New Year

Where Is It? All over Thailand

When Does It Happen? Every year from April 13 to April 15

SONGKRAN FESTIVAL

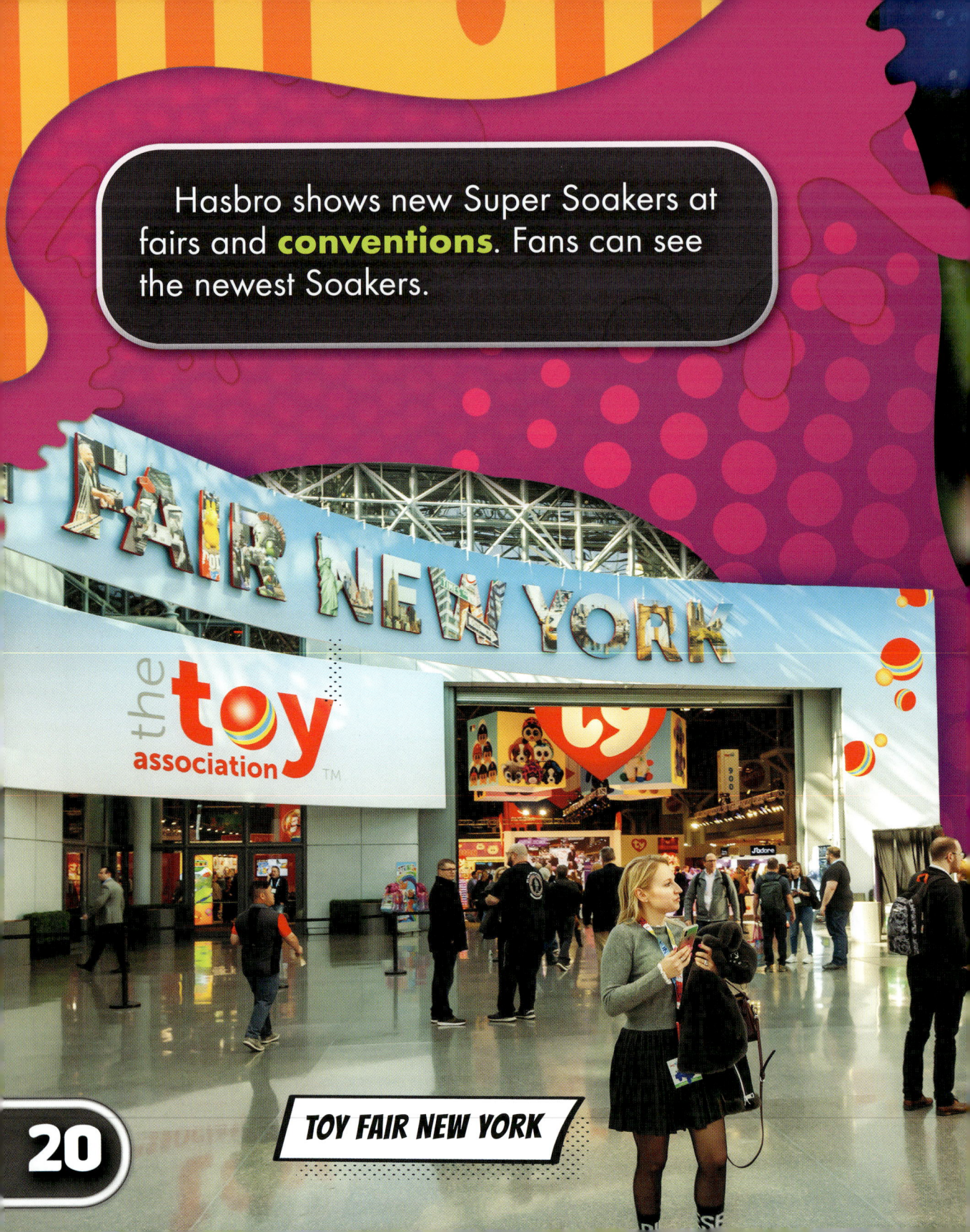

Hasbro shows new Super Soakers at fairs and **conventions**. Fans can see the newest Soakers.

TOY FAIR NEW YORK

Super Soakers are always a blast!

Glossary

ads—notices and messages that tell people to do or buy things

conventions—events where fans of a subject meet

corporation—a business or organization

firearms—weapons from which a shot is made with gunpowder

invented—made for the first time

nozzles—short tubes that help direct or speed up the flow of fluids

scopes—devices that help people view things from far away

trigger—the part of a Super Soaker that is pressed to spray water from it

To Learn More

AT THE LIBRARY

Castro, Rachel. *Lonnie Johnson.* Chicago, Ill.: Norwood House Press, 2020.

Raatma, Lucia. *Lonnie Johnson: NASA Scientist and Inventor of the Super Soaker.* North Mankato, Minn.: Capstone, 2020.

Sommer, Nathan. *Nerf Blasters.* Minneapolis, Minn.: Bellwether Media, 2022.

ON THE WEB

Factsurfer.com gives you a safe, fun way to find more information.

1. Go to www.factsurfer.com.

2. Enter "Super Soakers" into the search box and click 🔍.

3. Select your book cover to see a list of related content.

Index

ads, 11
beginnings, 7
Constant Pressure System, 12
conventions, 20
drums, 14
fairs, 20
Fortnite, 17
Hasbro, 14, 20
history, 6, 7, 8, 9, 10, 11, 12
Johnson, Lonnie, 6, 7, 8, 9, 10
Larami Corporation, 9, 11
name, 10, 11
Nebraska, 6, 7
Nerf blasters, 9, 14
nozzles, 12
Nyantakyi, Gabriel, 18
Pennsylvania, 18
Power Drencher, 10
pump, 6, 7
Reid, Chris, 17
sales, 11
scopes, 14
Songkran Festival, 18, 19
timeline, 13
trigger, 8
types, 14, 15
water, 7, 8, 10, 12, 14, 16, 18
water fight, 16, 18, 19
Waterarms Over Firearms, 18
XP Soakers, 12

The images in this book are reproduced through the courtesy of: Brittany McIntosh/ Bellwether Media, cover (hero); Josh Brink/ Bellwether Media, cover (small images), back cover, pp. 2, 15 (DinoSquad), 15 (Fortnite), 23; anthony marsh/ Alamy, pp. 4 (child), 5 (child); kubais, pp. 4-5 (water stream); Office of Naval Research/ Wiki Commons, pp. 6-7; Charles Sykes, p. 8; Islandstock/ Alamy, p. 9; John Bazemore/AP/Shutterstock, p. 10; ullstein bild/ Getty Images, p. 11; Mouse in the House/ Alamy, pp. 12 (top), 13 (logo); Robert Neapolitan / Mr. Darby's Emporium, p. 12 (bottom); John F. Williams/ Wiki Commons, p. 13 (top Lonnie); EQRoy, p. 13 (bottom); The Washington Post/ Getty Images, p. 14; urbanbuzz/ Alamy, p. 15(FreezeFire); Keith Homan, p. 15 (Scatter Strike); Anadolu/ Getty Images, pp. 16, 21; Sean P. Aune, p. 17; Christopher Evens/ Alamy, p. 18; SOE ZEYA TUN/ Alamy, p. 19; rblfmr, p. 20.